Why Struggle?

life is too short to wear tight shoes

Barbara J. Faison

BALBOA.
PRESS

A DIVISION OF HAY HOUSE

Balboa Press books may be ordered through booksellers or by contacting:

Balboa Press
A Division of Hay House
1663 Liberty Drive
Bloomington, IN 47403
www.balboapress.com
1 (877) 407-4847

Because of the dynamic nature of the Internet, any web addresses or links contained in this book may have changed since publication and may no longer be valid. The views expressed in this work are solely those of the author and do not necessarily reflect the views of the publisher, and the publisher hereby disclaims any responsibility for them.

The author of this book does not dispense medical advice or prescribe the use of any technique as a form of treatment for physical, emotional, or medical problems without the advice of a physician, either directly or indirectly. The intent of the author is only to offer information of a general nature to help you in your quest for emotional and spiritual well-being. In the event you use any of the information in this book for yourself, which is your constitutional right, the author and the publisher assume no responsibility for your actions.

Any people depicted in stock imagery provided by Thinkstock are models, and such images are being used for illustrative purposes only. Certain stock imagery © Thinkstock.

Print information available on the last page.

ISBN: 978-1-5043-7937-3 (sc)
ISBN: 978-1-5043-7938-0 (e)

Balboa Press rev. date: 04/25/2017

Acknowledgments

To God, The Creator of all things...Words can't express my gratitude for the blessings in my life.

To my amazing, awesome, wonderful husband, TD, you are the best gift I have ever received.

To my parents, Moses and Lorene Faison, you made me feel treasured, valued and worthy of all the abundance in the universe.

To my brother, Tony, and his wife, Patricia, thank you for the love and support you all continue to give me through all of my life experiences.

To my niece, April Faison and nephew, Byron Faison, I am honored to be your aunt.

To all of my family and friends who have supported this effort and all of my creations. I honor you and appreciate you for helping me on this journey.

To all my teachers and the students that have honored me with your presence, I am grateful.

To my ancestors who walked the path ahead of me and still guide me in spirit, I am forever indebted for all that you endured.

Dedication

Mom and Dad, how blessed I was to have had you as my parents. You all should have taught classes on how to help parents teach their children how to navigate life. You gave me roots and wings and loved me through it all. And most importantly, you all knew how to parent to me as an adult.

TD, you are my love, my sweetheart, and such an indescribable presence in my life. Thank you for being the best husband and partner I could ever imagine. I look forward to our dances together as husband and wife.

For April Faison and Byron Faison, you are inspiration for me to continue to find love in all I do.

For Dewayne Robinson and Tyriel Robinson, I look forward to the journey and memories we will continue to create.

Your spirits touched me and I honor your memory:

Annie Lorene Jackson Faison

Moses Cornelius Faison

Ethel Glover

Bishop (Zack) Berry

Willie B. Jackson

Willie B. Jackson, Jr.

Estelle Jackson

Angela Greene

Curtis Jackson

William Jesse (Max) Williams, Jr.

Adisa Masomakali

Ronda Paramoure

Thomas Paramoure

Alice Frazier

Gregory Pratt

Harold Boone

Barbara Goggi

Phillip Hawkins

Georgia Chester

Helen Glover

Jennifer (Judy) Walden

Contents

About This Book

Greetings!

In 1999, I published the original printed version of this book, **Why Struggle? life is too short to wear tight shoes** because I was searching. I was searching for a connection that I knew existed, and I couldn't figure out what it was. I had questions running around in my mind from, "how did the world begin?" to "why are we here?", "why am I here?" Specifically, "what is this journey called life about?" and "what is my purpose?"

I had always been a curious child. I had thoughts, questions, ideas, and insights at a young age. I struggled because I felt that I did not fit in. **Why Struggle?** was my way of making sense of all the stuff going on in my life and life in general. I felt like I was on a constant roller coaster ride. I was struggling and searching. From my twenties through my forties, I went to different churches, I went to psychics, I studied astrology, I studied

Buddhism and more. I didn't become a devotee of any of these studies; I simply wanted to know what they were about and to have an understanding of them so I could gain an understanding of me and this thing called life.

One moment I would be ecstatic and filled with pure joy then in another moment I would feel devastated. I went in search of some understanding of life and what it was all about. How do you deal with all of the ebbs and flows, the ups and downs? Back then, I came to the conclusion that life was _____. The blank was filled in based on how you felt at that moment. Whatever you experienced was how you felt life was. Your experiences of life were based on whatever emotions you felt at the time. If you were feeling good, you might say life was fantastic, great or amazing. If you didn't feel good, you might say life was horrible, painful or tragic. In one year, my maternal grandmother, my paternal grandfather, and my father died (two weeks after my grandfather). I was meditating on sort of regular basis and journaling enough to have these tools to reach for when I experienced these profound losses. I am so grateful I had started some type of practice to keep my life grounded.

It's been about 18 years since **Why Struggle?** the book was published. The beautiful thing about life is that when you have a strong foundation, you can build on that foundation and continue to build. Spiritual practices like meditation, mindfulness, and prayer give me a strong foundation for my life. The initial book was a very important part of my personal and spiritual growth, just as this new endeavor for the e-book and audio book continues to allow me to Learn, Evolve, and Grow (LEG). My personal beliefs and life philosophies are the same, and I've added a few more since I've lived a lot more life.

My beliefs and life philosophies are:

- **Be Loving.** Love is the most powerful, healing, transformative power. Being loving is the answer to most situations.
- **Be truthful.** I must find my personal truth and what brings me joy and peace.
- **Move forward**. Everything happens for a reason. Many times I will never know why specific things happen, I must move forward anyway.
- **Be Forgiving.** Learn to forgive myself and others, quickly. There are no mistakes – only learning experiences.
- **Be Open.** I am a student and teacher in the school of life. Teachers are everywhere, and I must be an open and willing student at all times. Usually, when I am the "teacher" I learn way more than I could ever teach.
- **Order is a natural law.** Everything happens in divine order.
- **Be Calm.** Calm and chaos are both mental choices, I can choose differently at any time.
- **Be Easy.** Life is about timing and FLOW (Feeling Loving Open Willing). I am learning to get out of the way more.

- **Be One.** We are all interconnected because we are one.
- **LEG.** My main purpose is to Learn, Evolve, and Grow (LEG) as much I can. Everything else will fall into place.
- **Be Still.** Time in silence and having spiritual practices such as meditation, radical forgiveness, journaling and tapping (Emotional Freedom Technique) are essential for my overall well-being.
- **Trust my PGS.** My Personal Guidance System (PGS) will lead, guide and direct me when I relax and get still enough to hearing its directions.

Who knew in 1999 I would be teaching meditation classes and be that lady that might say to you..."I have a message for you." There is no way on earth I would have had that insight back then. It all started with questions and wanting answers. It all started with wanted to live a better life. It all started with simply not wanting to struggle. Struggling is a choice. Life is what you decide it will be regardless of the emotions you experience. I have learned that taking time to still helps me get clear and make better choices.

I've learned to ask important questions to help me continue to move forward in life. How do I feel right now? Am I struggling right now, if so why? If I am struggling, I remember that struggling is a choice and I ask myself if I really want to take that emotional rollercoaster ride that might be the next step. I've learned to BREATHE deeply and often in order to come back to right now.

What can I do **right now** to feel better? Breathe. Maybe listening to a song or playlist or taking a walk can help me have a different feeling. Do I really need to call someone or can I figure things out myself? Why am I struggling at this moment? Just breathing and saying to myself or out loud, "all is well and things are always working out for me calms me down."

If you are reading or listening to this book, I want you to know that I appreciate you. This journey we call life is truly what YOU decide it will be. Allow yourself to be open to possibilities. Feel and experience the emotions as they show up. Smile and know that you have all you need in this world because you are here and all is in divine order.

I hope you will find this book nourishing – for your soul and your adventure through life. For me, the meaning of life is to - **Live, Love, Learn, Grow, and Share.**

Today, life is **an adventure.** Enjoy the journey and remember...

Why Struggle? Life is too short to wear tight shoes

Develop a Belief System

What do you believe about yourself? Your abilities? Your family? Your beliefs are like seeds planted in soil – when nourished in the proper environment, seeds grow into beautiful foliage. As children, our belief system is based on the world we live in. Once we are grown, we must get clear about what works best for us as an adult.

As you learn, evolve, and grow, your belief system may change. Give yourself room to grow and change as you have life experiences. We all have life experiences that cause us to question what we believe. Be sure to take note of these experiences and check in with your personal guidance system (PGS) as you continue to live your life.

What you believe will manifest in your life, positively or negatively. Understanding and living by your belief system is part of the foundation of knowing who YOU really are. Be open and willing to question what is serving who you are at every stage of life.

What you believed as a child may no longer be what you believe as you are a maturing adult.

Practice: Think of the expressions you heard as a child. Filter through them and keep the ones you truly believe. Use these beliefs as a foundation for your future actions and continue to expand and create your own belief system.

Affirmation: I believe there is order in the universe and I am where I should be at this time.

Know Yourself

As children, the people in our intimate circle of adults defined our identities. The labels we receive as children often stay with us as young adults. As we move into adulthood we must discover who we are, separate from those labels. We must determine our own likes, dislikes, wants and needs.

What are your passions? When was the last time you really had fun? Try new adventures and note the things you like and dislike. Make discovering yourself a monthly, weekly or daily activity. Give yourself permission to get to know yourself. Give yourself permission to change. Give yourself permission to grow.

Remember we are constantly changing, so who you are today will not be who you will be in ten years, twenty years or fifty years. Your likes and dislikes may also change as you learn, evolve and grow.

Practice: Take one day to be completely spontaneous and discover what you enjoy. Wake up with no set agenda and let your day unfold. Take notes of what you enjoyed.

Affirmation: I discover myself at all stages of life.

Embrace Change

You probably got up this morning and got dressed. You may have showered, brushed your teeth, eaten breakfast, driven to work, read the newspaper, and had a cup of coffee or tea. You have already been through at least six changes. Every moment is a new change, every second is different from the last one. Change is a natural part of the life cycle. Learning to embrace change is a major step toward peace of mind.

Imagine seeing an old friend whom you loved dearly and giving him/her a loving hug. Think of this image the next time you have to handle a major change in your life. Picture yourself opening your arms and welcoming the opportunity to grow. Change will show up at your door regardless of how you feel about it. Learn to open the door and welcome your new friend, CHANGE, with a warm embrace.

Practice: Think of all the things that change in one hour. If you are having difficulty accepting change, repeat the affirmation, "I am open and willing to accept change in my life."

Affirmation: I trust the process of life and I easily flow with change.

Slow Down

When was the last time you did anything without rushing? We can reach out and touch people in numerous ways including the phone, email, and social media. Technology offers our society such wonderful enhancements to daily living that we sometimes forget to slow down. We get up with our smartphones, cuddle with them and go to bed with them and sometimes we allow them to dictate all of our daily activities.

Technology is not human and has no discretion or judgment. Remember to disconnect from technology to fully engage in life and with people. Set personal boundaries around the time you spend on the phone, computer or tablet. Be sure to schedule or factor in time for relaxation and down time.

Commit to turning off the phone and enjoying the beauty around you. If you are with someone, enjoy time with a human; the technology will be there after you are done.

Practice: Choose a time to spend alone in nature. Take a walk and slow down, breathe the air and feel the sun against your skin. Slow down and give every moment your undivided attention.

Affirmation: I allow my mind, body, and spirit to slow down and be at peace.

This Moment

Stop. What are you doing right now? What you are doing right now is this moment. If you are reading or listening to this book, be in the moment. Pay attention to what is NOW. THE PRESENT MOMENT!

If you find your thoughts drifting back to the past or into the future, STOP and BREATHE. Breathe in and breathe out. Conscious breathing connects you with the present moment.

Feel all the emotions life has to offer – joy, pain, sorrow, happiness, peace, etc. The past is over. No matter what is happening, I guarantee that you will feel another emotion before you even realize it.

The future is not certain. You only have this moment. There will never be another moment like this one.

Practice: For one day, take the time to notice things around you. Be in each moment by stopping during the day to be aware of your breath. Breathe in and breathe out. Take a slow drive, look at nature, and revel in the beauty that surrounds you.

Affirmation: I feel all the elements of this moment and revel in the beauty of life.

Let It Go/Move On (LIGMO)

A few moments ago you might have been reading about the importance of silence or knowing the stages of grief. Time has passed and you are in another moment. This moment is the only thing you can do anything about. Events that have taken place cannot be changed.

Imagine walking around with a hot coal in your hand every time you find yourself holding on to the past. Would you want to carry a hot coal for seconds, minutes, or hours?

Accept the past for what it is – OVER. Accept what you have now as a gift, the PRESENT.

Practice: Think about a situation you can't seem to let go of. Sit in a quiet place. Ask your divine source to help you let go of the situation. Use the affirmation, "I let go of the past, I move forward with love in my heart."

Affirmation: I move forward in my life with joy.

Celebrate Everything!

Life is a journey. A trip. A deck of cards. Life defies a single definition because moment by moment, life changes. Life is different for each person every moment. Just as life changes, we change and grow based on our experiences. Treat yourself to something because you met a goal – celebrate!

Life simply is. Being alive is cause for celebration! Take a moment to think of a reason to celebrate. Treat yourself to something because you met a goal – celebrate! Perhaps you didn't use your cell phone when you were having a meal. CELEBRATE!

Every day find reasons to be grateful for life and celebrate! Sometimes it's just as simple as not beating yourself up about something you did. Now that is cause for a major celebration.

Practice: Think about the music you've listened to, the movies you've seen, the friends in your life and how they may have changed over the years. Treat yourself to something you enjoy. You deserve it.

Affirmation: I celebrate life and I am grateful for all my life experiences.

Self-Confidence Is Like the Weather

Some days I wake up feeling fantastic! Some days I don't feel as great when I wake up.

It's okay. Life is still happening all around. Self-confidence and self-esteem are like the weather. Hot, cold, cloudy or rainy – the weather is always changing. Some days we feel great about ourselves. Other days, we want to crawl back under the covers and wait for a new day.

When I'm having a particularly challenging day, I go to bed as early as I can. Often times, if I can, I will take a nap. There is something about sleeping that mentally shifts my energy and helps me move forward. I am comforted by knowing that tomorrow is a new day and there's a 50/50 chance the sun will shine.

Always know there are other people having stormy days just like you. Look yourself in the mirror and be grateful to be alive.

Practice: Look at yourself in the mirror daily. Look for all the lines, wrinkles, and perfections. Affirm aloud, "I love all of me - body, mind, and spirit."

Affirmation: I accept myself for the beauty I have to offer and I share myself with the world.

You are Not Alone

Life is challenging. How often have you thought you were the only person going through something difficult? You are not alone. We are afraid to share our fears and stories because we don't want to be judged by others. People are not as strong, confident, and wise as they seem. Other people are afraid, lonely, and going through tough times, too.

You may think you are the only person experiencing whatever you are feeling. Trust me, there is someone else experiencing the same fear, anxiety, pain, hurt or joy you are feeling. Remember, no matter what is happening, you are NOT alone.

My mom used to remind me to have a "talking partner." She said it was important to have someone you could be vulnerable with to express your fears or concerns. You will instinctively know who you can share your thoughts with at these times. Trust your intuition and find a talking partner.

Practice: Think of something you feel self-conscious about. Share this feeling with someone you trust and respect. As you become more comfortable, share more of your feelings with other people.

Affirmation: Life is joyous. I am surrounded by love.

Love Yourself

As babies, we are full of adventure and curiosity. Our parents and other adults in our intimate circle set our first boundaries. As we grow older, we must set new boundaries.

How do you treat yourself? Do you take time for yourself? Do people treat you how you want to be treated? If you don't like your answers, set new boundaries for yourself and adjust them as needed. As you begin to change, people will adapt their behavior.

If you aren't pleased with the way others treat you, look at how you treat yourself. Can you look yourself in the mirror and say I love you? Can you write yourself a love letter and list all your wonderful traits? Start with those simple acts and become comfortable with expressing your love for yourself to you.

Self-love and acceptance are important for your well-being and growth. Make loving yourself an active practice by paying attention to how you feel in different situations. Listen to your intuition, your Personal Guidance System (PGS) and feel yourself fall deeper and deeper in love, with you.

Practice: Think about how you want to be treated. If you don't like how people treat you, think of someone you respect and think of how others treat him/her. Use this as a guide to adjust your boundaries. Practice assertiveness as others approach you.

Affirmation: I accept and love myself for who I am.

"You Can't Make Anyone _____"

Wouldn't it be nice to have people do what we want them to do all day long? Good luck with that. We live in a society of free will. Every day we make choices. Each person takes a path that will be filled with learning experiences for that individual.

You can't make anyone do anything they don't want to do. The only behavior you can control is your own. A reminder of this is watching a two-year-old or any child have a tantrum. The child will stop when ready, no matter what anyone tries to say or do to him/her.

We can't control anyone as much as we may think we can. Learn to accept people for who they are, not who you want them to be. Learn to manage your ability to respond to others and check in with yourself. Learn to step back and check your expectations.

Practice: Before you ask anyone to change his/ her behavior, think about your expectations. Is the change for your benefit because it would make you more comfortable? How would you feel if someone wanted you to change your behavior?

Affirmation: I accept people for who they are in my life.

Shoulda, Coulda, Woulda ...NOT

I **should** go to the gym. I should eat healthier.

I **could** have done more if I knew my mother was ill.

I **would** have spent more time with her.

If you **SHOULD**, do it. If you **CAN**, do it.

If you **WOULD** have, it would be done already.

Decide what you really want to do and **DO IT**.

If you need help, find a person or group of people to help you remain accountable for what you want to do. Accountability is a great tool; learn to use it and watch your shoulda, coulda, and woulda's disappear.

Practice: Think of five important things that you should, could or would have done. Think about how you can turn those thoughts into actions. If you can't act on these things, release those thoughts and move on.

Affirmation: I accept responsibility for my life.

Know the Stages of Grief

Life is a cycle. We are born. We live. We die. Death is as natural as living. Recognizing and accepting the laws of nature can help us live more in the present moment. As we learn to accept our lives and live without struggling over the inevitable, we can truly appreciate the gift of life.

Denial, anger, bargaining, depression and acceptance are the stages of grief. The time for each stage is as unique as your fingerprint. Experience the emotions as they arise and be gentle with yourself at this time.

Remember we may also experience grief when we make changes in our lives such as a change in a relationship, moving to a new city or a change in your work environment. A loss is a loss, give yourself permission to grieve as you feel necessary.

Practice: Remember when someone you loved died and how you felt. Think about the emotions you felt.

Were they denial, anger, bargaining, depression, and acceptance?

Affirmation: I accept the flow of life. Peace of mind is mine.

Think like A Child

Do you remember the last time you laughed until you cried? When was the last time you were really curious about how something worked? When was the last time you looked at something and were amazed? A young child has a unique outlook on life and can help you remember how awesome life is.

Children are born with a natural curiosity about everything. Having children in your life can help you become a more creative problem solver, learn to accept the inevitable, and laugh at yourself more. Young children help you remember a sense of awe.

Being around children and younger people allow you to see life through different eyes. Take time to really watch, listen and learn from the young people in your life. Wisdom is not limited to a certain age.

Practice: Spend the day with a child between the ages of two and six years old. Go to a park with no specific agenda. Observe the child and notice how they are amazed at the simple things that adults have taken for granted. The next time you need to solve a problem, think like a child.

Affirmation: I celebrate the spirit of the child in my heart.

Ask for Help

This can be a tough one. In this "I can do it all" world, asking for help may seem like a sign of weakness or an inability to manage your time effectively. My mother would say, "You can help no one, especially yourself, if you are worn out and dog-tired."

I used to be so busy, I had a change of clothes I would keep in the car. I would be gone all day. I had to rethink where I wanted to focus my TEE (Time, Energy and/or Effort). Everything in life requires some form of TEE. I looked at what I was doing and where I was spending my time and limited my major activities to three a day. I factored in where I need to go, how long it will take me, and the order of what I need to do. If I needed help, I checked with someone who was able to help me.

Sometimes we need to slow down and reassess how we truly want to spend our time. If you think you have too much to do, or not enough time to do what is needed – you do! Learn to say no or ask for help.

Don't forget to reciprocate and help others when your time frees up.

Practice: Look at your list of things to do as you plan your day. If there is anything you need help with, ask someone to help you with those items.

Affirmation: I allow people to help me when I am in need.

Fear is Real

Fear is real. If you perceive something as fearful, your body will respond based on that perception. Whatever you tell yourself, the mind keeps score of that item like a scorekeeper at a game. Mind your mind. Train your brain. Pay attention to what you think about. The mind is a powerful tool that we can use more to our advantage.

Can you educate yourself about your fears? Are there other people with the same fears? Perhaps you can find a group online and connect with others who have the same concerns. Can you work with them to overcome the issue?

Maybe you can sit quietly and ask for guidance on why you are fearful. It might be helpful to start writing down thoughts about your fears. Take small steps toward managing your fears and celebrate your progress. Develop an action plan to manage your fears and move in that direction.

Practice: Think of something you fear. Sit in a quiet place, close your eyes and try to visualize the incident that was the catalyst for the fear. Affirm aloud, "I let go of the past. I move forward with love in my heart."

Affirmation: I am alive to the joys of living and embrace life.

Acceptance

"Grant me the serenity to change the things I can, the courage to accept the things I cannot change and the wisdom to know the difference." These words by Reinhold Niebhur can change your life if you choose to live them.

Acceptance isn't resignation. Acceptance is receiving what has been presented. When my grandfather and father died within two weeks of each other, I had to accept that as a fact. Denying the obvious would not change what happened. I felt all the emotions that would be expected in that situation.

Allow yourself to accept things so you can move forward with your life. Remember you don't want to walk around with a hot coal in your hand, so learn the art of accepting each moment and moving forward.

We will never understand everything that happens. When something happens, accept the event as a fact.

Let the next moment come into play and be present to that moment.

Practice: When someone does something that you don't agree with, repeat the affirmation, "I cannot change the way that person is. I accept the beauty they have to offer." Try this for one day, one week, and one month; then make it a life practice.

Affirmation: I am open and accepting of all people.

Forgive

We are all human and have all done things we are not proud of. We have all been hurt by someone. We must learn to forgive others for their betrayals and indiscretions. We must learn to forgive ourselves for being hurt, ashamed or damaged by someone else's actions. Forgiveness is one of the keys to freedom and peace of mind.

Research ways to practice forgiveness. I learned a technique, Radical Forgiveness, which has changed my life for the better. This approach allows me to reflect on myself, the situation and gives me ways to move forward. I've learned to appreciate situations through forgiveness that I would never have expected. Being open to forgiveness is freeing.

Find what works for you so you can move forward and release the energy that holds you back when you have not forgiven yourself and/or others.

Practice: Sit in a quiet place and ask your divine source to open your heart to forgive all parties involved. Visualize a white light surrounding everyone and send thoughts of love and forgiveness.

Affirmation: I forgive myself and all others and allow peace and love to flow into our lives.

Be Quiet

How often have you been drawn into conversations or arguments with people who enjoy debating? Some people know certain words or expressions will trigger a response and will try to bait you into a discussion which may turn into an argument. Yes, you can always say something, but do you really NEED to say anything? Is a response absolutely required?

There are many times no response is required. Stop, breathe and take a moment to connect with your intuition, your Personal Guidance System (PGS). Silently ask yourself if anyone benefits from your response in that moment.

Be cautious with your words and save your comments for those will value what you say.

Practice: Give your next conversation your undivided attention. Turn your body to the person, look them in the eyes and open your ears to hear his/her words. Pause for 3 seconds before responding. If a response is not required, say nothing.

Affirmation: I speak with power and purpose.

Be Silent

A few minutes of silence as a daily practice can reduce stress as we calm our minds and thoughts from a hectic day. Simply take a few minutes before you start your day and lie in bed and observe what you hear, how you feel and what you sense. Check in with yourself and your body before you start the day.

I've recently consciously decided to not use my smartphone for at least 10 – 15 minutes after I wake up to allow my mind, body and spirit to wake up and listen for guidance. When possible I also enjoy the silence of the house without the television or music. Being silent for periods of time will give you a new appreciation for the power of spoken words and sounds.

It took me years to truly understand how powerful silence can be. Now, I relish, crave and look for ways to immerse myself in silence. Like much of life, learning to be silent is a practice. Regular meditation has helped me become as comfortable with silence as I am with speaking.

Silence can be deafening if you are unfamiliar with its sound. Silence can scare you if you are unaware of its value. Silence can be your friend if you embrace it.

Practice: Find a consistent time when you can spend at least 10 uninterrupted minutes. Sit in a comfortable position, close your eyes and take a few deep breaths. BE still. Be alone with your thoughts and hear what is inside you during these peace-filled moments.

Affirmation: Harmony embraces me and I am surrounded by love.

Be Adventurous!

One definition of adventurous is inclined or willing to engage in a bold, usually risky undertaking. An adventure can be as simple as going to a movie alone or buying a book from an unknown author. Do something different **often.** Buy music from an unknown artist. Take a dance class. Say hello to a stranger.

One of the ways I started being adventurous was to drive a different way home from work. I would turn down a street and find my way home based on that turn. Keep in mind, this was before GPS devices were the norm. I also started buying something new to try when I went grocery shopping. Trying different foods from is a great way to increase your adventurous nature.

Venture out of your comfort zone to find people who are open-minded and willing to try new things. By venturing out more, you will continue to learn and grow and become more adventurous. The more we try new things, the less we will stress when something different happens.

Practice: Go to a function alone and introduce yourself to at least three people you don't know.

Affirmation: I am open to new ideas and experiences.

Be Yourself

I am very fortunate to have a great circle of friends. When you love yourself and understand who you are and what you bring to the world, you only want to be you. I am a great Barbara but not a good Suzanne or any other friend. Suzanne is my oldest friend, we've been friends over 50 years. I love her dearly for who she is.

How many times have you thought, "If they really knew me, they probably wouldn't like me?" How long have you pretended to be someone else simply to please other people? Pretending to be someone you aren't takes a toll on us mentally, physically and spiritually.

If you are alive, you have something to offer the world. Your presence in the world is not a mistake nor is it random. Know you are special and learn to love yourself and appreciate your unique qualities.

Stop pretending to have it all together if you don't. Be yourself and others will learn to accept the real you. The people who are intended to be around you will love you for who you are.

Practice: Take a day for yourself and do exactly what you want to do with no explanation to anyone. See where your thoughts and ideas lead you.

Affirmation: I am at peace in this moment. I love myself just as I am.

Be Grateful

I say "thank you, God" all day long. I feel so blessed and grateful for my life and the people in my life. Even when things are not a great as I would like them to be, I'm still grateful for I know I have the ability to move forward.

Do you have all five senses? **BE GRATEFUL.**
Can you walk? **BE GRATEFUL.**
Are you able to eat? **BE GRATEFUL.**
Do you have shelter? **BE GRATEFUL.**
Do you have clothing for your body? **BE GRATEFUL.**
Can you read? **BE GRATEFUL.**
Can you think and express yourself? **BE GRATEFUL.**

Being grateful has now been scientifically proven to be a stress buster. Grateful people are more optimistic and reap the health benefits of the practice. Cultivate the practice of appreciation and look for what you are learning from your experiences. Simply say out loud throughout the day, "thank you."

Practice: Do you have clothing, food, and shelter? What about sight, touch, smell, taste, hearing? Be grateful if you do. The next time you begin to feel ungrateful, think of all the basic things in life you have to give thanks for.

Affirmation: I am grateful and appreciate my life.

Be Kind

Think about the last kind thing you did for someone – something that was unexpected. Are you smiling? You should be. Being genuinely kind to someone can lift your spirits and take your focus off what you don't have.

We all want to be loved and appreciated. Kindness transcends culture and language. In a world where our differences seem to separate us, a gesture of kindness is one way to acknowledge our sameness.

If you are in line at the store and the person behind you has only a few items, why not let that person check out ahead of you? Such an effort is a simple kindness that might have major benefits for you and the person you helped.

Practice: Pledge to do one kind thing a week. Increase it to one thing every other day. Increase your kind acts to once a day and watch your life and heart bloom.

Affirmation: I openly share joy and love to all.

Money is Not Evil

Money is not the root of evil. Money or currency is a representation of what people think will make them happy. Being rich will set you free from all the demons of the world, right?

Does money truly motivate you, or it is the freedom that having money provides? If we lived in a society where having a golden duck was the expected level of being rich, would everyone try to find as many golden ducks as they could? What is a lot of money? Does money equate to happiness?

Investigate your beliefs about money and take time to get clear about your relationship to money. You may have to do go deeper into your family dynamics to gain more insight.

Practice: Imagine you won the lottery for the amount of money you feel would set you up for life. Think of all the things you would do with your winnings. After thinking of everything, what's next?

Affirmation: I understand and accept the purpose of money in my life.

Learning... Evolving... Growing (LEGging baby!) = PRACTICE

When I initially wrote *Why Struggle?* I was convinced that life was about discovering yourself. I even named my publishing company In Search of Publications based on that belief. The longer I live, the more I believe that we are here to discover, create and accept ourselves at each stage of life. Aren't humans lucky? We can make a different choice anytime we decide. We don't have to have a "bad day;" we can choose to have a "bad moment." Again, even a bad moment is a conscious choice. Notice the use of the words: choose, conscious, decide. I believe words are powerful, and I choose mine carefully.

I have always been very curious. I have always been a creative thinker. I have always enjoyed sharing information with others. My curious nature has propelled me down very interesting roads and for that, I am truly grateful. One of my traveled paths has been the road of meditation and creative visualization. For years I dabbled with quiet time and struggled with making it a part of my daily practice until 1995. I was so desperate for peace of mind that I pledged to spend at least 10 minutes in silence in the morning. In a few weeks, I was more relaxed and able to accept things I could not change. I tried many forms of meditation and began using visualization exercises to add more focus. I usually sense things or hear thoughts versus seeing images. The daily practice has helped me become calmer and more confident. Meditating daily greatly changed my life. Simply put, meditation makes me a better person for me and for the people around me. Taking a few minutes to sit and be still allows me to gain clarity and make better choices.

It is not during meditation that I receive my ideas; it is because of the daily practice of meditation that I am more open to sense, hear or feel something that may be helpful. The practice of meditating regularly opens you up to opportunities you might not see otherwise. When I wake up in the morning, I usually have tons of ideas running around in my head. I know it is because I plant seeds at night before retiring and simply by doing meditation or deep breathing, I have a garden of ideas waiting for me to share them with the world.

My morning ritual has changed over the years based on where I am and what I choose to focus on. Generally, I include some type of meditation, either guided, silent or walking along with verbal affirmations and gentle stretches. I have also started a practice of life scripting where I proactively write about my desires in a journal. Most mornings I walk Lacee, my furry sister (12-year-old Yorkipoo) who moved in with me when my mother came to live with me in May 2012. I've moved away from so much planning and now I set clearer intentions and move in a specific direction based on my intention versus sticking to a specific plan. As a former planner, I am still working on this. I have also learned that just when you think you have some control over life, life changes and you have to adjust and go with the flow. I had no idea how much my life would change on the morning of September 11, 2011.

At 7:40 AM, I received a call from my mother who lived in Albany, GA, which was about 200 miles from where I lived. My mother has never been an early riser so my heart initially jumped when I saw her name on the caller ID. I immediately knew something was wrong. Mom told me she saw blood in her stool. I took several deep breaths and started to tell her what to do. I don't remember the details, but I do recall that at one time she stopped talking. Later I found out that mom had passed out. I called 911 from my home in Stone Mountain, GA and was patched through to 911 in Albany, and an ambulance was sent. Mom's neighbors were amazing and helped my brother and I stay calm while we both packed to get to Albany. I know my years of meditating helped me get through that experience.

After several lengthy hospitalizations over four months, Mom settled into a rehabilitation center in Atlanta and moved into my home three months later. Prior to that call on 9/11 my mother had never had a major illness, so experiencing pain was new to her. My mother maintained her beautiful spirit and energy over three years during some very challenging times. After years of avoiding dialysis, mom decided to start the treatments in September 2014. In December 2014 I married TD Robinson and I now have 2 sons, Dewayne (12) and Tyriel (22). My life went from being a single woman to having a mother, her dog, a husband, two sons and all that goes along with these blessings.

I believe my mother wanted to see me in my new roles as a wife and mother. I felt her loving spirit watching over me as she adjusted to being away from her home, church and all she knew back in Albany. My friends LOVED my mom and she truly blessed so many people while she was on this earth. I had the chance to learn how to cook food I had no interest in when mom tried to teach me as a young girl. My husband is glad I learned how to make many southern dishes like collard greens, turnip greens, speckled butter beans mixed with black-eyed peas and others. Mom used to make a great sweet tea with cinnamon and mint, she should have sold the recipe to someone. I had an appreciation for being in the kitchen that I would never have had as a teen. Thank you God for this blessing.

Taking mom to doctor's appointments, dialysis (3 times a week), grocery shopping, shopping, holidays and just daily living are memories that will stay with me forever. Mom would always have to know the names of everyone that she met when she was at the doctor's office or in the hospital. She knew how to make you feel special and radiated such love and warmth. As much as she didn't enjoy dialysis, she embraced it and was a bright light at the center with the patients and staff. We had a rhythm to life and things were flowing smoothly. I went into the office twice a week and took her to dialysis on the other days, and my brother also helped with the scheduling. Mom rarely complained about anything, it just wasn't a part of her nature. She had mentioned that she was tired of dialysis a few weeks prior to her final hospitalization.

I went home right after work on July 29, 2015. Listening to my PGS is what got me to go home instead of going to my usual sound vibration meditation class. When I arrived home mom was on the sofa and I asked how she was feeling. Mom admitted she was still having a pain in her neck/shoulder area. We went to the emergency room and she was admitted to the hospital that night and remained in the hospital in Cardiac Care Unit (CCU) as they tried to stabilize her blood pressure prior to her surgery.

While she was in the CCU mom made more friends with the doctors, nurses, nursing assistants, other patients' family members, and the cleaning staff as she learned and remembered their names. The doctors and fellows that checked on her were amazed at her energy, spirit, and enthusiasm for life. Her surgeon called her a "young 80" and agreed to the surgery after evaluating and watching her zest for life.

On Wednesday, a week after she was admitted to the hospital mom had surgery. She had complications while in surgery and we were told she coded four times. Her surgeon was thoughtful, compassionate and honest with us as he told us that they were unable to close her stomach and the 24 hours after the surgery would be crucial for her recovery. He told us he would be very honest with us as they monitored her and she was put on 24-hour dialysis. Slowing down and paying attention is crucial to life and I am glad I was able to notice all that happened next.

On Friday morning I went to walk Lacee as we do daily unless the weather is inclement. Lacee refused to walk. Talk about timing, I'd left my cell phone and as soon as I went back in the house the surgeon called to say he needed to speak with us. I knew what he was going to say. I called my brother and waited for him in the CCU conference room. The hospice nurse and social worker came into the waiting room and I had to smile when I saw their names, the same as two of my co-workers and spelled the same way. Kelley and Meredith.

My mother was surrounded by her family and a caring team as she transitioned due to complications after surgery on August 7, 2015. The next day, Lacee was back to her usual active self and we walked the neighborhood. I was on the phone with a friend talking about how grateful I was to have had mom with me for three years when a beautiful butterfly landed on my wrist. I smiled. I felt it was mom's spirit letting me know she was okay. Many of my friends also saw butterflies around this time, often by their doorway.

My mother, "the sage of life", touched many lives and her beautiful presence is still felt when I hear her words of wisdom from my family and friends. I am eternally grateful for having my mother with me for over three years as I learned how to navigate my new life as a wife, caregiver, and mother. Listening to mom's loving and encouraging words were like a salve on a wound when I felt discouraged or unclear of which direction to go. Slow down, take your time, stop running around like a lizard were some of my favorites from mom. Mom's dog, Lacee, is a beautiful reminder of her spirit every day as we head out on our daily walks.

My Spiritual Practices

Slowing down and paying attention to what is right in front of me has truly opened me up to more opportunities and grace. Silence, meditation, listening to music, walking, and forgiveness are some of my spiritual practices that help me stay grounded. It's called a practice because it is doing something regularly or constantly as an ordinary part of your life. When I stray from my daily meditation, affirmation, and prayers, I immediately feel it. That's why it is called a "daily" spiritual practice, not a "whenever I feel like doing it" practice.

Can you imagine your favorite sports team just showing up for the game without practicing first, and expecting to play well and win? Not at all, practice is part of the process. Over the years my spiritual practice has evolved based on what I have going on in my life. The key thing is to find what works for you as a practice and to PRACTICE.

My current practices are Meditations, Affirmations, and Prayers and whatever moves me at the time.

57

My M.A.P. - MEDITATIONS

Years of living alone conditioned me to enjoy quiet in the morning. I rarely turned on the television when I was getting dressed for the day. My meditations vary now based on what is happening in my world. There are times I sit and focus on specific areas of my life and visualize, sometimes I sit and enjoy the quiet of nature. I go with whatever flow I feel like that day. I also may listen to various meditations from other sources such as meditationoasis.com, davidji.com, kellyhowell.com, Oprah and Deepak 21 Day Meditation challenge and Omvana. There are so many resources for meditation, these are some of my favorites.

Walking is one of my favorite types of meditations now. As Lacee and I walk, I am drawn to the beauty all around me from the trees, flowers, butterflies to the sun shining down on my skin. Lacee has become one of my daily teachers. Some days as we walk the neighborhood, she will slow down and sniff the grass or flowers she sees every day as if it is her first time seeing them. I listen to the birds as we walk the neighborhood and I feel the gentle touch of the wind on a crisp fall morning. When I see butterflies in my area I smile and say, "hi mom." Witnessing God through birds, butterflies and other amazing creatures is its own meditation.

My M.A.P. - AFFIRMATIONS

An affirmation is a statement you believe or assert to be true. I believe every thought is an affirmation and every thought is a prayer. Since I am blessed to be able to think, why not think and be as positive as possible?

It is human nature to remember negative things, so affirmations can be a way to practice moving past what you don't want in your life. More scientific research is showing that choosing positive affirmative thoughts is beneficial to your overall well-being.

If I desire something, I focus my feelings and thoughts on what I desire through thinking, writing, and speaking about it. It is important to, "Train your brain. Mind your mind. Pay attention to what you think about." Using affirmations are a great way to train your brain. Affirmations allow me to auto correct myself whenever I am not focusing on the best and what I truly want.

My current daily affirmation is:

I have strength, stamina, endurance, and flexibility. I manage my life well. I trust that the right people and resources present themselves at the right time and I recognize them immediately. I take time during my day to be still so I can get clear and make the best choices for me at all times. No matter how I feel or how things appear, I know that all things are working out for my highest and greatest good. And I am grateful.

Here are some of the standard affirmations I use or have used. I also use various sources for reference when I am looking for a specific area to focus my thoughts. Louise Hay, Iylana Vanzant, Catherine Ponder, Edwene Gaines and Joyce Rennolds are some of my favorite authors for affirmations as well as other life-affirming practices.

- ☯ All is well.
- ☯ I am divinely protected at all times.
- ☯ I trust the process of life. All I need is taken care of. I am safe.
- ☯ I am calm. I am safe. All is well.
- ☯ I let go of the past, I move forward with love in my heart.

- I handle all of my experiences with wisdom, with love, and with ease.
- I am filled with excellent health, energy, and vitality.
- The universe loves me and supports all my endeavors.

Affirmations are portable, personal, positive and present tense. Affirmations may be written, spoken and/or thought during your day at any time. No one has to know what you are thinking, just think your affirmations, especially if you are beating yourself up over something or over nothing. I say many of my affirmations as I'm walking the dog in the morning. I also use affirmations to keep my thoughts and feelings on what I want in my life.

I think it is human nature to think about what is not right so anything I can do to focus on what I desire is helpful. Affirmations are a great way to practice thinking about what you want. It's one way to reprogram your thinking.

My M.A.P. - PRAYERS

When I wake up and before I open my eyes, I pray. I take a deep breath and say out loud, "Thank you, God." TD and I each say a prayer out loud before we begin the day. I pray all day, every day. My standard prayer throughout the day is, "Thank you, God." Saying thank you during the day (even in what appears to be troubling times) keeps me in the present moment and allows me to remember that in another moment, I'll feel another emotion. Sometimes I will say my prayers silently or aloud as I am walking the dog and I also say them while I'm getting dressed. I go with how I feel and below is an example of what I may say.

Dear God,

Thank you for waking me up this morning with my sight, taste, touch, smell, hearing, and intuition. I am grateful for another day on this earth to be an ambassador of your love. Keep me tuned in for the places I can best serve all.

I am grateful for my amazing husband and wonderful family and friends who love, accept, and support me.

Thank you for my ancestors who paved the way for me to go the places I go, do the things I do and be the person I am.

Thank you for the many blessings in my life. Thanks for all the experiences I have and the presence of mind to remember that all is in divine order. I know my path is for me and the right people and circumstances will present themselves at the right time.

Please bless the countries, leaders, and families in need of help and continue to lead and guide me in all my endeavors.

Please bless the families that need your love and support at this time. (I will list specific names I have at this time.)

Meditation/Visualization Exercises

So what is meditation? One of my favorite descriptions of the meditation process is that meditation is mental hygiene. Every day we brush our teeth and shower or bathe before leaving the house. We make sure we are properly groomed before presenting ourselves to the world. Meditation, a form of mental hygiene, is a way to prepare my mind for the day by allowing me to connect with my inner guidance. Meditating regularly is like muscle training; the more I meditate, the more in tuned to life I become. My mental focus and clarity gets stronger just as my physical muscles get stronger when I exercise them.

Imagine your mind is like a bowl, open and ready to receive. As we go through our day, our minds are filled with thoughts, images, and sounds - many of those we have no control of based on our environment. Unless we take the time to manage these things, our bowls begin to overflow. Science now confirms that we can manage our minds and have a major impact on our lives by simply slowing down and paying attention more. It's important that we take the time to feed our mind just as we feed our body. Paying attention to what we listen to, who we spend our time with and what we feed our mind is crucial for love and self-acceptance.

Meditation is one way that allows you to manage your emotions and thoughts. Visualization is similar to having a focused daydream. When you visualize, you are the main character in your movie, mentally designing how you want to see things unfold. Taking a two or three minutes to think specifically about something you want to see in your life is a practice that is very beneficial.

In my meditation time, I often reflect on what is important to me so I can start my day with a clear mind. Meditating daily helps me manage the stuff I allow in my bowl. The most important element of any practice is consistency. I am more focused because I begin every day from a place of peace and gratitude. Meditation is a process. The more I meditate, the more comfortable I become with the process. The breathing practice that accompanies meditation gives me an opportunity to be present to what is happening, right now. This meditative time allows me to become more aware of what is happening in my life and world. I think of meditation as a form of mental focus. I have discovered that it is because of the silence, not in the silence, I gain more clarity.

Imagine you discovered a new flavor of ice cream that you didn't know you liked until you tried it. That's how meditation feels to me. I didn't know I liked pistachio until I tried it. And now, I really enjoy that flavor of ice cream. I would even try to order it or buy it if available. Meditation is like that for me now. I find ways during my day to find moments to be present by meditating or taking time to connect with my breath or just paying attention more.

Once you decide to start meditating, your experience will vary each time you meditate. Be gentle with yourself and allow what happens to happen and just be present to whatever comes up. This is not a test or a goal that needs to be completed. Developing a practice is committing to being there and present, your willingness is all that is required. Make your practice as formal or informal as you choose. The most important thing is that you decide to meditate. The reminders below may help you connect with creating your practice, these are not required, just things to consider:

- Make the commitment to meditate for ten minutes a day. If you've decided to have a partner, confirm the day you will start and how you will follow up with each other when you are done.
- Find or create your sacred space where you can be uninterrupted for at least ten minutes.
- Turn off all phones, TVs, computers and other distractions and decide to be present.
- Give yourself permission to indulge in this form of self-care. You deserve it!
- Appreciate any thoughts that may come up during your practice and return to whatever your focus is, breath, mantra or phrase, to bring you back to your breath.
- When you are paying full attention to whatever you are doing, that is a form of meditation - walking alone, crocheting, knitting, eating and only eating, gardening, etc.
- Be present to whatever happens in your practice; it will be unique to you.
- You may want to have a notebook or paper to write any observations after your practice.

Experiment with various things until you are comfortable. As you begin to use your mind as the amazing tool it is, you will grow and notice your level of confidence grow and your doubts lessen.

The following pages are samples of meditation and visualization exercises that will help you learn to focus on your breath. If you don't have time for 5 – 10 minutes of meditations as recommended below, see if you can stop and connect with your breath for 3 – 5 minutes. You can stop, close your eyes and take 3 deep breaths and use the thought, "I am" on the inhale and "here now" on the exhale. When you are comfortable with your breathing, try the meditation and visualization exercises.

Remember – ETE – Enjoy The Experience!

Note: Feel free to practice these with or without a timing device.

Breathing Practice

Sit comfortably with your back straight if possible. Close your eyes and begin to become aware of your breath.

Simply breathe in and breathe out. Pay attention to your breath as you breathe in and out.

Just breathe in and breathe out.

Breathe in and breathe out.

Feel the air moving through your nose and through your chest. Just breathe in and breathe out.

Continue breathing and being aware of your breath and use this breathing technique throughout your day.

Try this practice for 5 minutes a day.

Purpose: To increase your awareness of breathing more consciously. Breath allows you to become aware of each moment.

Deep Breathing Practice

Sit comfortably with your back straight if possible. Gently close your eyes and begin to become aware of your breath. Simply breathe in and breathe out. Pay attention to your breath as you breathe in and out and allow your body to settle into this practice.

Just breathe in and breathe out. Place your hands on your stomach as you continue to breathe.

On your next in breath take a deep breath in while pressing your belly out as if you are trying to push your belly button out as far as you can. On your next exhale, press your belly button back into place.

Continue pressing out your belly button on your exhale and pressing your belly button back into place on the inhale.

Once you are comfortable with this belly breathing begin counting to 3 on the in breath as you expand your stomach. Hold your breath for a count of 3, then contract your stomach for the count of 3. You should feel more air moving through your body.

Continue breathing deeply for up to ten minutes. When you are ready to return to the present moment, open your eyes and allow your breath to return to normal.

Continue using this deep breathing technique during your day or whenever you want a reminder to be in the present moment. This deep breathing is also very helpful to reduce stress or anxiety.

Purpose: Reminder to be present. Deep breathing helps with reducing anxiety or stress.

Awareness Meditation

Choose a place where you can be undisturbed for a least 10 minutes daily. Make this your sacred space and decorate this area with items that are soothing, calming or beautiful to you, if you desire. Sit comfortably, close your eyes and become aware of your breath.

Simply breathe in and breathe out. Pay attention to your breath as you breathe in and out and allow your body to settle into this practice.

Just breathe in and breathe out. Place your hands on your stomach as you continue to breathe.

On your next in breath take a deep breath in while pressing your belly out as if you are trying to push your belly button out as far as you can. On your next exhale, press your belly button back into place.

Continue pressing your belly button out on your exhale and pressing your belly button back into place on the inhale.

Keep breathing in and breathing out pressing your belly button out on your exhale and in on the inhale.

In your mind, begin to count backwards from 20 as you continue to breathe. Your thoughts might wander; allow them to wander and continue breathing. Simply enjoy the silence of this moment and continue to breathe in and out.

After you have reached one, open your eyes and allow your breath to return to normal.

Purpose: To increase your awareness of how your thoughts race through your mind and to become comfortable with silence.

Thoughtful Meditation

Choose a place where you can be undisturbed for a least 10 minutes daily. Make this your sacred space and decorate this area with items that are soothing, calming or beautiful to you. Sit comfortably, close your eyes and become aware of your breath.

Simply breathe in and breathe out. Pay attention to your breath as you breathe in and out and allow your body to settle into this practice.

Just breathe in and breathe out. Place your hands on your stomach as you continue to breathe.

On your next in breath take a deep breath in while pressing your belly out as if you are trying to push your belly button out as far as you can. On your next exhale, press your belly button back into place.

Continue pressing your belly button out on your exhale and pressing your belly button back into place on the inhale.

Keep breathing in and breathing out.

Slowly begin to focus on your thoughts on your bodily sensations. As thoughts run through your mind, name them. If you feel restless, name it. I feel restless.

Continue to name the feelings as they run through your mind. When the feelings or thoughts go away, return to being aware of your breath. Continue breathing for up to ten minutes. When you are ready to return to the present moment, open your eyes and allow your breath to return to normal.

Purpose: To increase your awareness of your bodily sensations and feelings, and to name your thoughts and feelings.

Visualization

Sit comfortably with your back straight if possible. Close your eyes and begin to become aware of your breath. Simply breathe in and breathe out. Pay attention to your breath as you breathe in and out and allow your body to settle into this practice.

Just breathe in and breathe out. Place your hands on your stomach as you continue to breathe.

On your next in breath take a deep breath in while pressing your belly out as if you are trying to push your belly button out as far as you can. On your next exhale, press your belly button back into place.

Continue pressing your belly button out on your exhale and pressing your belly button back into place on the inhale.

Once you are comfortable with this belly breathing begin counting to 3 on the in breath as you expand your stomach. Hold your breath for a count of 3, then contract your stomach for the count of 3. You should feel more air moving through your body.

Continue pressing your belly button out on your exhale and pressing your belly button back into place on the inhale.

Think of a specific desire or goal. Picture the environment where you are as you are completing the goal.

What does the place look like? What sounds do you hear? Who is there with you, and what are they doing? How does it smell?

This is your movie and you are the star of the show. What are you wearing? What are you doing? How are you interacting with the others?

See yourself going through the process of achieving your goal in your movie. When you've completed your goal, place the picture inside a beautiful pink bubble and see the bubble and your goal drift up into the sky. You are releasing your attachment and allowing love to surround your desires.

Slowly open your eyes and bring your awareness to your present location.

Purpose: To see yourself successfully achieving your goals and releasing your attachment to the results.

Now What?

Now, it's time for you to step out of your comfort zone. Be adventurous! Sign up for a continuing education class. Take a trip by yourself. Make a list of all the things you have always wanted to do and start doing those things...do them alone, or find other people to share your fun. In the technology-focused world, we live in, Google and the internet provides an abundance of ways to connect with like-minded people. Why not check into meetup groups that share your same interests?

Slow down and pay attention MORE. Paying attention is one of the most powerful and inexpensive forms of personal development. It is crucial to take time to be in nature, to notice it, to revel in it and express appreciation for it. Taking time to be still can be as simple as staying in the car an extra five minutes, sitting in the bathroom longer and even turning off the radio as you drive/ride to your destination.

Simple ways to be still are all around. Start to pay attention and be where you are when you are there.

When you explore beyond your usual boundaries, you magically meet people who are doing the same thing. There is order in the universe, and when the time is right, all the elements fall into place. When you create the habit of doing something new or different you open up a new world of experiences.

We are all students and teachers in the school of life. We are where we should be at this time, place and space. Life is ____.

We are here to: Live... Love... Learn... Grow... Share.

Live each moment to the fullest and ...

Why Struggle? life is too short to wear tight shoes

About the Author

 Barbara J. Faison believes we are all students and teachers in the school of life, and being open to learning, evolving and growing is a way to stop struggling with life.

Barbara educates, inspires, and enlightens with her unique perspective on being on purpose wherever you are. Instead of struggling, take a few minutes each day to be still, gain clarity and make better choices. Being loving and compassion can help us all learn to struggle less.

Barbara is an Electrical Engineering graduate of Tuskegee University and a member of Toastmasters International.

Barbara is a meditation and mindfulness ambassador and author of the audio program, ***"Be Still: Learn to Meditate in 10 Minutes a Day."***

Connect with Barbara on social media:

www.barbarafaison.com
barbarajfaison/facebook
barbarafaison/twitter
barbarafaison/Instagram
barbarafaison/youtube
barbarafaison/snapchat